Fort...
or
Prayer Consecration

The Answer To Your Prayers

Daily Devotions for Spiritual Growth

Pastor Tony Simmons

KINGDOM JOURNEY PRESS
A DIVISION OF KINGDOM JOURNEY ENTERPRISES
WOODBRIDGE, VA

i

DEDICATION

Forty Days of Prayer Consecration *is dedicated to:*

Rachel Simmons,
My Wife

Brandon and Carlton Simmons,
My Sons

James and Martha Simmons,
My Parents

Bishop Norman O. Harper
My Pastor and Mentor

Elder Alex Anderson and Intervarsity Fellowship,
My Mentor

Elder Luther R. Hinsley, Sr.,
My Pastor

Superintendent Kenneth W. Boddie,
My Pastor

The late Bishop Chandler David Owens,
My Bishop

Bishop Carlos Simon,
My Friend

• • •

Nice

CONTENTS

INTRODUCTION..vii

HOW TO IMPLEMENT FORTY DAYS OF PRAYER CONSECRATION...........ix

Proverbs 3:6 1

1Timothy 2:1-2 5

1 Thessalonians 5:17..9

1 Peter 5:7 13

1 John 5:14-15..17

Isaiah 26:3 21

Mark 11:24...25

Matthew 6:33 29

Matthew 7:7 33

Proverbs 18:10 37

John 14:14..41

Hebrews 11:6 45

Jeremiah 29:11 49

Psalm 121:1..53

Philippians 4:8 57

Psalm 84:2..61

Psalm 50:15..65

Psalm 25:14..69

Luke 11:1-4 73

Jeremiah 32:27 77

Romans 8:32 81

Isaiah 65:24..85

Psalm 9:10..89

Psalm 34:8..93

John 15:4-5...97

James 5:16..101

Psalm 91:1..105

Philippians 4:19 109

Psalm 20:7..113

Psalm 63:1-2 117

John 1:12..121

Acts 12:5 125

* * *

v

John 15:14...129
Psalm 145:8..133
Romans 12:2 137
Acts 3:1 141
Psalm 103:2..145
2 Corinthians 5:17..149
Psalm 86:5..153
Jeremiah 9:23-24..157
ABOUT THE AUTHOR 161
ABOUT KINGDOM JOURNEY PRESS..163

INTRODUCTION

Forty Days of Prayer Consecration

Whatever the need is of a moment, the answer is in God. Whatever we are feeling or desiring, all hope lies in God. If there was ever a time in our lives to get closer to God, that time is NOW.

Simply stated, we can get close to Him by talking (and listening) to Him in prayer. Jesus put prayer before every work to hear from His Father. If Jesus prayed, surely we should pray often and without ceasing. We stay plugged into God by submitting to be a person of prayer.

Forty days of prayer will give you a hunger for God. Forty days of prayer will make you thirst for God. Forty days of prayer will empower you with the presence of God.

God delights in those who worship Him in their prayer life. Allow Him to soak you with His presence during this "consecrated" time.

HOW TO IMPLEMENT FORTY DAYS OF PRAYER CONSECRATION

There are three core areas that should be practiced daily during the 40 Day Prayer period:

1. Read the Scriptures and Prayer for each day, several times during the day;

2. Read the Daily Prayer List and pray everything on the list each day; and

3. Apply and document in the Prayer Journal what God has taught you during Prayer each day.

A special thanks to Bishop Norman O. Harper for teaching me structured ministry.

Forty Days
of
Prayer Consecration

<u>Day 1</u>

<u>Prayer & Scripture</u>

Proverbs 3:6

In all thy ways acknowledge him, and he shall direct thy paths.

Prayer for Today

Father, in the name of Jesus, help me to be reminded daily to allow You to direct every area of my life.

Daily Prayer List

Pray for your personal relationship with the Lord as your Savior.

Pray for God to fill you with His Presence today.

Pray that God helps you to stay dedicated to His word and to honor His commandments by keeping His word.

Pray that your resources will be used for God's glory.

Pray to serve God throughout your day and through the opportunities that He provides.

Pray for your family, friends and the people you work with and meet.

Pray about everything that you are involved with throughout your day.

Pray for people needing healing and deliverance.

Pray for people in the mission fields, in prisons and in schools of learning.

Pray for God's protection.

Pray for those in authority (Pastors, Ministry Leaders, Community/Political Leaders, Supervisors, and the President).

Pray for peace in the various nations of the world.

Pray that God will bless your hands as He expands your territory for His glory.

Pray for a spirit of thanksgiving in everything.

<u>Prayer Journal</u>

_____
_____
_____
_____
_____
_____
_____
_____
_____
_____
_____
_____
_____
_____
_____
_____
_____
_____
_____
_____
_____
_____
_____
_____

<u>Day 2</u>

<u>Prayer & Scripture</u>

1Timothy 2:1-2

1I exhort therefore, that, first of all, supplications, prayers, intercessions, and giving of thanks, be made for all men;

2For kings, and for all that are in authority; that we may lead a quiet and peaceable life in all godliness and honesty.

Prayer for Today

Father, in the name of Jesus, I pray for all that are in authority. Allow Your glory to head each person, that they might fulfill Your purpose.

Daily Prayer List

Pray for your personal relationship with the Lord as your Savior.

Pray for God to fill you with His Presence today.

Pray that God helps you to stay dedicated to His word and to honor His commandments by keeping His word.

Pray that your resources will be used for God's glory.

Pray to serve God throughout your day and through the opportunities that He provides.

Pray for your family, friends and the people you work with and meet.

Pray about everything that you are involved with throughout your day.

Pray for people needing healing and deliverance.

Pray for people in the mission fields, in prisons and in schools of learning.

Pray for God's protection.

Pray for those in authority (Pastors, Ministry Leaders, Community/Political Leaders, Supervisors, and the President).

Pray for peace in the various nations of the world.

Pray that God will bless your hands as He expands your territory for His glory.

Pray for a spirit of thanksgiving in everything.

Prayer Journal

_____

_____

_____

_____

_____

_____

_____

_____

_____

_____

_____

_____

_____

_____

_____

_____

_____

_____

_____

<u>Day 3</u>

<u>Prayer & Scripture</u>

1 Thessalonians 5:17

Pray without ceasing.

Prayer for Today

Father, in the name of Jesus, help me to pray about everything throughout my day.

Daily Prayer List

Pray for your personal relationship with the Lord as your Savior.

Pray for God to fill you with His Presence today.

Pray that God helps you to stay dedicated to His word and to honor His commandments by keeping His word.

Pray that your resources will be used for God's glory.

Pray to serve God throughout your day and through the opportunities that He provides.

Pray for your family, friends and the people you work with and meet.

Pray about everything that you are involved with throughout your day.

Pray for people needing healing and deliverance.

Pray for people in the mission fields, in prisons and in schools of learning.

Pray for God's protection.

Pray for those in authority (Pastors, Ministry Leaders, Community/Political Leaders, Supervisors, and the President).

Pray for peace in the various nations of the world.

Pray that God will bless your hands as He expands your territory for His glory.

Pray for a spirit of thanksgiving in everything.

<u>Prayer Journal</u>

_____
_____
_____
_____
_____
_____
_____
_____
_____
_____
_____
_____
_____
_____
_____
_____
_____
_____
_____
_____
_____
_____
_____

Day 4

Prayer & Scripture

1 Peter 5:7

Casting all your care upon him; for he careth for you.

Prayer for Today

Father, in the name of Jesus, I cast all of my cares on You because it is Your desire to handle them.

Daily Prayer List

Pray for your personal relationship with the Lord as your Savior.

Pray for God to fill you with His Presence today.

Pray that God helps you to stay dedicated to His word and to honor His commandments by keeping His word.

Pray that your resources will be used for God's glory.

Pray to serve God throughout your day and through the opportunities that He provides.

Pray for your family, friends and the people you work with and meet.

Pray about everything that you are involved with throughout your day.

Pray for people needing healing and deliverance.

Pray for people in the mission fields, in prisons and in schools of learning.

Pray for God's protection.

Pray for those in authority (Pastors, Ministry Leaders, Community/Political Leaders, Supervisors, and the President).

Pray for peace in the various nations of the world.

Pray that God will bless your hands as He expands your territory for His glory.

Pray for a spirit of thanksgiving in everything.

<u>Prayer Journal</u>

_____
_____
_____
_____
_____
_____
_____
_____
_____
_____
_____
_____
_____
_____
_____
_____
_____
_____
_____
_____
_____
_____
_____

<u>Day 5</u>

<u>Prayer & Scripture</u>

1 John 5:14-15

14And this is the confidence that we have in him, that, if we ask any thing according to his will, he heareth us:

15And if we know that he hear us, whatsoever we ask, we know that we have the petitions that we desired of him.

Prayer for Today

Father, in the name of Jesus, I have confidence that you hear me because I worship You. I know that You have blessed me according to Your will. I appreciate that You answer my petitions.

<u>Daily Prayer List</u>

Pray for your personal relationship with the Lord as your Savior.

Pray for God to fill you with His Presence today.

Pray that God helps you to stay dedicated to His word and to honor His commandments by keeping His word.

Pray that your resources will be used for God's glory.

Pray to serve God throughout your day and through the opportunities that He provides.

Pray for your family, friends and the people you work with and meet.

Pray about everything that you are involved with throughout your day.

Pray for people needing healing and deliverance.

Pray for people in the mission fields, in prisons and in schools of learning.

Pray for God's protection.

Pray for those in authority (Pastors, Ministry Leaders, Community/Political Leaders, Supervisors, and the President).

Pray for peace in the various nations of the world.

Pray that God will bless your hands as He expands your territory for His glory.

Pray for a spirit of thanksgiving in everything.

<u>Prayer Journal</u>

_____

_____

_____

_____

_____

_____

_____

_____

_____

_____

_____

_____

_____

_____

_____

_____

_____

_____

_____

_____

<u>Day 6</u>

<u>Prayer & Scripture</u>

Isaiah 26:3

Thou wilt keep him in perfect peace, whose mind is stayed on thee: because he trusteth in thee.

Prayer for Today

Father, in the name of Jesus, I confess that you are my peace and I trust in You. When I think on You, You bring me peace and I thank You for that.

Daily Prayer List

Pray for your personal relationship with the Lord as your Savior.

Pray for God to fill you with His Presence today.

Pray that God helps you to stay dedicated to His word and to honor His commandments by keeping His word.

Pray that your resources will be used for God's glory.

Pray to serve God throughout your day and through the opportunities that He provides.

Pray for your family, friends and the people you work with and meet.

Pray about everything that you are involved with throughout your day.

Pray for people needing healing and deliverance.

Pray for people in the mission fields, in prisons and in schools of learning.

Pray for God's protection.

Pray for those in authority (Pastors, Ministry Leaders, Community/Political Leaders, Supervisors, and the President).

Pray for peace in the various nations of the world.

Pray that God will bless your hands as He expands your territory for His glory.

Pray for a spirit of thanksgiving in everything.

<u>Prayer Journal</u>

_____
_____
_____
_____
_____
_____
_____
_____
_____
_____
_____
_____
_____
_____
_____
_____
_____
_____
_____
_____
_____

Day 7

Prayer & Scripture

Mark 11:24

Therefore I say unto you, What things so ever ye desire, when ye pray, believe that ye receive them, and ye shall have them.

Prayer for Today

Father, in the name of Jesus, I thank You for Your word which declares that I can have whatever I desire if I believe that I will receive it.

Daily Prayer List

Pray for your personal relationship with the Lord as your Savior.

Pray for God to fill you with His Presence today.

Pray that God helps you to stay dedicated to His word and to honor His commandments by keeping His word.

Pray that your resources will be used for God's glory.

Pray to serve God throughout your day and through the opportunities that He provides.

Pray for your family, friends and the people you work with and meet.

Pray about everything that you are involved with throughout your day.

Pray for people needing healing and deliverance.

Pray for people in the mission fields, in prisons and in schools of learning.

Pray for God's protection.

Pray for those in authority (Pastors, Ministry Leaders, Community/Political Leaders, Supervisors, and the President).

Pray for peace in the various nations of the world.

Pray that God will bless your hands as He expands your territory for His glory.

Pray for a spirit of thanksgiving in everything.

<u>Prayer Journal</u>

_____

_____

_____

_____

_____

_____

_____

_____

_____

_____

_____

_____

_____

_____

_____

_____

_____

_____

_____

_____

_____

<u>Day 8</u>

<u>Prayer & Scripture</u>

Matthew 6:33

But seek ye first the kingdom of God, and his righteousness; and all these things shall be added unto you.

Prayer for Today

Father, in the name of Jesus, I ask that You be first in my life. I seek You and Your righteousness. Thank you for blessing me. I honor You for the peace you have given me.

Daily Prayer List

Pray for your personal relationship with the Lord as your Savior.

Pray for God to fill you with His Presence today.

Pray that God helps you to stay dedicated to His word and to honor His commandments by keeping His word.

Pray that your resources will be used for God's glory.

Pray to serve God throughout your day and through the opportunities that He provides.

Pray for your family, friends and the people you work with and meet.

Pray about everything that you are involved with throughout your day.

Pray for people needing healing and deliverance.

Pray for people in the mission fields, in prisons and in schools of learning.

Pray for God's protection.

Pray for those in authority (Pastors, Ministry Leaders, Community/Political Leaders, Supervisors, and the President).

Pray for peace in the various nations of the world.

Pray that God will bless your hands as He expands your territory for His glory.

Pray for a spirit of thanksgiving in everything.

<u>Prayer Journal</u>

_____

_____

_____

_____

_____

_____

_____

_____

_____

_____

_____

_____

_____

_____

_____

_____

_____

_____

_____

_____

_____

_____

Day 9

Prayer & Scripture

Matthew 7:7

Ask, and it shall be given you; seek, and ye shall find; knock, and it shall be opened unto you:

Prayer for Today

Father, in the name of Jesus, I thank You for Your word which declares that I can seek and knock and You will open doors for me.

Daily Prayer List

Pray for your personal relationship with the Lord as your Savior.

Pray for God to fill you with His Presence today.

Pray that God helps you to stay dedicated to His word and to honor His commandments by keeping His word.

Pray that your resources will be used for God's glory.

Pray to serve God throughout your day and through the opportunities that He provides.

Pray for your family, friends and the people you work with and meet.

Pray about everything that you are involved with throughout your day.

Pray for people needing healing and deliverance.

Pray for people in the mission fields, in prisons and in schools of learning.

Pray for God's protection.

Pray for those in authority (Pastors, Ministry Leaders, Community/Political Leaders, Supervisors, and the President).

Pray for peace in the various nations of the world.

Pray that God will bless your hands as He expands your territory for His glory.

Pray for a spirit of thanksgiving in everything.

<u>Prayer Journal</u>

_____

_____

_____

_____

_____

_____

_____

_____

_____

_____

_____

_____

_____

_____

_____

_____

_____

_____

_____

_____

_____

<u>Day 10</u>

<u>Prayer & Scripture</u>

Proverbs 18:10

The name of the LORD is a strong tower: the righteous runneth into it, and is safe.

Prayer for Today

Father, in the name of Jesus, I thank You for Your awesome name. Your name is my strong tower and Your name protects me.

<u>Daily Prayer List</u>

Pray for your personal relationship with the Lord as your Savior.

Pray for God to fill you with His Presence today.

Pray that God helps you to stay dedicated to His word and to honor His commandments by keeping His word.

Pray that your resources will be used for God's glory.

Pray to serve God throughout your day and through the opportunities that He provides.

Pray for your family, friends and the people you work with and meet.

Pray about everything that you are involved with throughout your day.

Pray for people needing healing and deliverance.

Pray for people in the mission fields, in prisons and in schools of learning.

Pray for God's protection.

Pray for those in authority (Pastors, Ministry Leaders, Community/Political Leaders, Supervisors, and the President).

Pray for peace in the various nations of the world.

Pray that God will bless your hands as He expands your territory for His glory.

Pray for a spirit of thanksgiving in everything.

<u>Prayer Journal</u>

<u>Day 11</u>

<u>Prayer & Scripture</u>

John 14:14

If ye shall ask any thing in my name, I will do it.

Prayer for Today

Father, in the name of Jesus, I count it all joy to ask for anything in prayer by Your name. Your name gives me access for You to bless my life.

Daily Prayer List

Pray for your personal relationship with the Lord as your Savior.

Pray for God to fill you with His Presence today.

Pray that God helps you to stay dedicated to His word and to honor His commandments by keeping His word.

Pray that your resources will be used for God's glory.

Pray to serve God throughout your day and through the opportunities that He provides.

Pray for your family, friends and the people you work with and meet.

Pray about everything that you are involved with throughout your day.

Pray for people needing healing and deliverance.

Pray for people in the mission fields, in prisons and in schools of learning.

Pray for God's protection.

Pray for those in authority (Pastors, Ministry Leaders, Community/Political Leaders, Supervisors, and the President).

Pray for peace in the various nations of the world.

Pray that God will bless your hands as He expands your territory for His glory.

Pray for a spirit of thanksgiving in everything.

<u>Prayer Journal</u>

_____
_____
_____
_____
_____
_____
_____
_____
_____
_____
_____
_____
_____
_____
_____
_____
_____
_____
_____
_____
_____

<u>Day 12</u>

<u>Prayer & Scripture</u>

Hebrews 11:6

But without faith it is impossible to please him: for he that cometh to God must believe that he is, and that he is a rewarder of them that diligently seek him.

Prayer for Today

Father, in the name of Jesus, I desire to please You. I lean and depend totally on You.

Daily Prayer List

Pray for your personal relationship with the Lord as your Savior.

Pray for God to fill you with His Presence today.

Pray that God helps you to stay dedicated to His word and to honor His commandments by keeping His word.

Pray that your resources will be used for God's glory.

Pray to serve God throughout your day and through the opportunities that He provides.

Pray for your family, friends and the people you work with and meet.

Pray about everything that you are involved with throughout your day.

Pray for people needing healing and deliverance.

Pray for people in the mission fields, in prisons and in schools of learning.

Pray for God's protection.

Pray for those in authority (Pastors, Ministry Leaders, Community/Political Leaders, Supervisors, and the President).

Pray for peace in the various nations of the world.

Pray that God will bless your hands as He expands your territory for His glory.

Pray for a spirit of thanksgiving in everything.

<u>Prayer Journal</u>

_____

_____

_____

_____

_____

_____

_____

_____

_____

_____

_____

_____

_____

_____

_____

_____

_____

_____

_____

_____

_____

_____

Day 13

Prayer & Scripture

Jeremiah 29:11

For I know the thoughts that I think toward you, saith the LORD, thoughts of peace, and not of evil, to give you an expected end.

Prayer for Today

Father, in the name of Jesus, I appreciate Your thoughts of peace towards me. It brings me joy to know that You have an excellent end for me.

<u>Daily Prayer List</u>

Pray for your personal relationship with the Lord as your Savior.

Pray for God to fill you with His Presence today.

Pray that God helps you to stay dedicated to His word and to honor His commandments by keeping His word.

Pray that your resources will be used for God's glory.

Pray to serve God throughout your day and through the opportunities that He provides.

Pray for your family, friends and the people you work with and meet.

Pray about everything that you are involved with throughout your day.

Pray for people needing healing and deliverance.

Pray for people in the mission fields, in prisons and in schools of learning.

Pray for God's protection.

Pray for those in authority (Pastors, Ministry Leaders, Community/Political Leaders, Supervisors, and the President).

Pray for peace in the various nations of the world.

Pray that God will bless your hands as He expands your territory for His glory.

Pray for a spirit of thanksgiving in everything.

<u>Prayer Journal</u>

_____

_____

_____

_____

_____

_____

_____

_____

_____

_____

_____

_____

_____

_____

_____

_____

_____

_____

_____

_____

_____

<u>Day 14</u>

<u>Prayer & Scripture</u>

Psalm 121:1

I will lift up mine eyes unto the hills, from whence cometh my help.

Prayer for Today

Father, in the name of Jesus, I look up to You because You are my help.

<u>Daily Prayer List</u>

Pray for your personal relationship with the Lord as your Savior.

Pray for God to fill you with His Presence today.

Pray that God helps you to stay dedicated to His word and to honor His commandments by keeping His word.

Pray that your resources will be used for God's glory.

Pray to serve God throughout your day and through the opportunities that He provides.

Pray for your family, friends and the people you work with and meet.

Pray about everything that you are involved with throughout your day.

Pray for people needing healing and deliverance.

Pray for people in the mission fields, in prisons and in schools of learning.

Pray for God's protection.

Pray for those in authority (Pastors, Ministry Leaders, Community/Political Leaders, Supervisors, and the President).

Pray for peace in the various nations of the world.

Pray that God will bless your hands as He expands your territory for His glory.

Pray for a spirit of thanksgiving in everything.

<u>Prayer Journal</u>

_____
_____
_____
_____
_____
_____
_____
_____
_____
_____
_____
_____
_____
_____
_____
_____
_____
_____
_____
_____
_____

<u>Day 15</u>

<u>Prayer & Scripture</u>

Philippians 4:8

Finally, brethren, whatsoever things are true, whatsoever things are honest, whatsoever things are just, whatsoever things are pure, whatsoever things are lovely, whatsoever things are of good report; if there be any virtue, and if there be any praise, think on these things.

Prayer for Today

Father, in the name of Jesus, I pray to You for the things that I should think on as Your word transforms my mind.

Daily Prayer List

Pray for your personal relationship with the Lord as your Savior.

Pray for God to fill you with His Presence today.

Pray that God helps you to stay dedicated to His word and to honor His commandments by keeping His word.

Pray that your resources will be used for God's glory.

Pray to serve God throughout your day and through the opportunities that He provides.

Pray for your family, friends and the people you work with and meet.

Pray about everything that you are involved with throughout your day.

Pray for people needing healing and deliverance.

Pray for people in the mission fields, in prisons and in schools of learning.

Pray for God's protection.

Pray for those in authority (Pastors, Ministry Leaders, Community/Political Leaders, Supervisors, and the President).

Pray for peace in the various nations of the world.

Pray that God will bless your hands as He expands your territory for His glory.

Pray for a spirit of thanksgiving in everything.

<u>Prayer Journal</u>

_____
_____
_____
_____
_____
_____
_____
_____
_____
_____
_____
_____
_____
_____
_____
_____
_____
_____
_____
_____
_____
_____

Day 16

Prayer & Scripture

Psalm 84:2

My soul longeth, yea, even fainteth for the courts of the LORD: my heart and my flesh crieth out for the living God.

Prayer for Today

Father, in the name of Jesus, my heart desires more of You. Help me to long for You always.

Daily Prayer List

Pray for your personal relationship with the Lord as your Savior.

Pray for God to fill you with His Presence today.

Pray that God helps you to stay dedicated to His word and to honor His commandments by keeping His word.

Pray that your resources will be used for God's glory.

Pray to serve God throughout your day and through the opportunities that He provides.

Pray for your family, friends and the people you work with and meet.

Pray about everything that you are involved with throughout your day.

Pray for people needing healing and deliverance.

Pray for people in the mission fields, in prisons and in schools of learning.

Pray for God's protection.

Pray for those in authority (Pastors, Ministry Leaders, Community/Political Leaders, Supervisors, and the President).

Pray for peace in the various nations of the world.

Pray that God will bless your hands as He expands your territory for His glory.

Pray for a spirit of thanksgiving in everything.

<u>Prayer Journal</u>

_____

_____

_____

_____

_____

_____

_____

_____

_____

_____

_____

_____

_____

_____

_____

_____

_____

_____

_____

_____

_____

_____

<u>Day 17</u>

<u>Prayer & Scripture</u>

Psalm 50:15

And call upon me in the day of trouble: I will deliver thee, and thou shalt glorify me.

Prayer for Today

Father, in the name of Jesus, I call on You because You always help me in my time of trouble.

<u>Daily Prayer List</u>

Pray for your personal relationship with the Lord as your Savior.

Pray for God to fill you with His Presence today.

Pray that God helps you to stay dedicated to His word and to honor His commandments by keeping His word.

Pray that your resources will be used for God's glory.

Pray to serve God throughout your day and through the opportunities that He provides.

Pray for your family, friends and the people you work with and meet.

Pray about everything that you are involved with throughout your day.

Pray for people needing healing and deliverance.

Pray for people in the mission fields, in prisons and in schools of learning.

Pray for God's protection.

Pray for those in authority (Pastors, Ministry Leaders, Community/Political Leaders, Supervisors, and the President).

Pray for peace in the various nations of the world.

Pray that God will bless your hands as He expands your territory for His glory.

Pray for a spirit of thanksgiving in everything.

Prayer Journal

_____
_____
_____
_____
_____
_____
_____
_____
_____
_____
_____
_____
_____
_____
_____
_____
_____
_____
_____
_____
_____
_____

<u>Day 18</u>

<u>Prayer & Scripture</u>

Psalm 25:14

The secret of the LORD is with them that fear him; and he will shew them his covenant.

Prayer for Today

Father, in the name of Jesus, I thank You for showing me Your secrets and Your way. Thank you for bonding me to Your covenant.

<u>Daily Prayer List</u>

Pray for your personal relationship with the Lord as your Savior.

Pray for God to fill you with His Presence today.

Pray that God helps you to stay dedicated to His word and to honor His commandments by keeping His word.

Pray that your resources will be used for God's glory.

Pray to serve God throughout your day and through the opportunities that He provides.

Pray for your family, friends and the people you work with and meet.

Pray about everything that you are involved with throughout your day.

Pray for people needing healing and deliverance.

Pray for people in the mission fields, in prisons and in schools of learning.

Pray for God's protection.

Pray for those in authority (Pastors, Ministry Leaders, Community/Political Leaders, Supervisors, and the President).

Pray for peace in the various nations of the world.

Pray that God will bless your hands as He expands your territory for His glory.

Pray for a spirit of thanksgiving in everything.

<u>Prayer Journal</u>

_____
_____
_____
_____
_____
_____
_____
_____
_____
_____
_____
_____
_____
_____
_____
_____
_____
_____
_____
_____
_____

Day 19

Prayer & Scripture

Luke 11:1-4

1And it came to pass, that, as he was praying in a certain place, when he ceased, one of his disciples said unto him, Lord, teach us to pray, as John also taught his disciples. 2And he said unto them, When ye pray, say, Our Father which art in heaven, Hallowed be thy name. Thy kingdom come. Thy will be done, as in heaven, so in earth. 3Give us day by day our daily bread. 4And forgive us our sins; for we also forgive every one that is indebted to us. And lead us not into temptation; but deliver us from evil.

Prayer for Today

Father, in the name of Jesus, thank you for giving us an example of prayer.

<u>Daily Prayer List</u>

Pray for your personal relationship with the Lord as your Savior.

Pray for God to fill you with His Presence today.

Pray that God helps you to stay dedicated to His word and to honor His commandments by keeping His word.

Pray that your resources will be used for God's glory.

Pray to serve God throughout your day and through the opportunities that He provides.

Pray for your family, friends and the people you work with and meet.

Pray about everything that you are involved with throughout your day.

Pray for people needing healing and deliverance.

Pray for people in the mission fields, in prisons and in schools of learning.

Pray for God's protection.

Pray for those in authority (Pastors, Ministry Leaders, Community/Political Leaders, Supervisors, and the President).

Pray for peace in the various nations of the world.

Pray that God will bless your hands as He expands your territory for His glory.

Pray for a spirit of thanksgiving in everything.

<u>Prayer Journal</u>

_____
_____
_____
_____
_____
_____
_____
_____
_____
_____
_____
_____
_____
_____
_____
_____
_____
_____
_____
_____
_____

<u>Day 20</u>

<u>Prayer & Scripture</u>

Jeremiah 32:27

Behold, I am the LORD, the God of all flesh: is there any thing too hard for me?

Prayer for Today

Father, in the name of Jesus, I know that no thing is too hard for You. There is no thing that You can not handle. All things are subject to You.

Daily Prayer List

Pray for your personal relationship with the Lord as your Savior.

Pray for God to fill you with His Presence today.

Pray that God helps you to stay dedicated to His word and to honor His commandments by keeping His word.

Pray that your resources will be used for God's glory.

Pray to serve God throughout your day and through the opportunities that He provides.

Pray for your family, friends and the people you work with and meet.

Pray about everything that you are involved with throughout your day.

Pray for people needing healing and deliverance.

Pray for people in the mission fields, in prisons and in schools of learning.

Pray for God's protection.

Pray for those in authority (Pastors, Ministry Leaders, Community/Political Leaders, Supervisors, and the President).

Pray for peace in the various nations of the world.

Pray that God will bless your hands as He expands your territory for His glory.

Pray for a spirit of thanksgiving in everything.

<u>Prayer Journal</u>

_____
_____
_____
_____
_____
_____
_____
_____
_____
_____
_____
_____
_____
_____
_____
_____
_____
_____
_____
_____

<u>Day 21</u>

<u>Prayer & Scripture</u>

Romans 8:32

He that spared not his own Son, but delivered him up for us all, how shall he not with him also freely give us all things?

Prayer for Today

Father, in the name of Jesus, I thank you for giving us Your Son who gave us eternal life.

Daily Prayer List

Pray for your personal relationship with the Lord as your Savior.

Pray for God to fill you with His Presence today.

Pray that God helps you to stay dedicated to His word and to honor His commandments by keeping His word.

Pray that your resources will be used for God's glory.

Pray to serve God throughout your day and through the opportunities that He provides.

Pray for your family, friends and the people you work with and meet.

Pray about everything that you are involved with throughout your day.

Pray for people needing healing and deliverance.

Pray for people in the mission fields, in prisons and in schools of learning.

Pray for God's protection.

Pray for those in authority (Pastors, Ministry Leaders, Community/Political Leaders, Supervisors, and the President).

Pray for peace in the various nations of the world.

Pray that God will bless your hands as He expands your territory for His glory.

Pray for a spirit of thanksgiving in everything.

<u>Prayer Journal</u>

_____

_____

_____

_____

_____

_____

_____

_____

_____

_____

_____

_____

_____

_____

_____

_____

_____

_____

_____

_____

_____

_____

<u>Day 22</u>

<u>Prayer & Scripture</u>

Isaiah 65:24

And it shall come to pass, that before they call, I will answer; and while they are yet speaking, I will hear.

Prayer for Today

Father, in the name of Jesus, I thank You for hearing me before I call. You know everything about me and my desires. I bless Your name.

<u>Daily Prayer List</u>

Pray for your personal relationship with the Lord as your Savior.

Pray for God to fill you with His Presence today.

Pray that God helps you to stay dedicated to His word and to honor His commandments by keeping His word.

Pray that your resources will be used for God's glory.

Pray to serve God throughout your day and through the opportunities that He provides.

Pray for your family, friends and the people you work with and meet.

Pray about everything that you are involved with throughout your day.

Pray for people needing healing and deliverance.

Pray for people in the mission fields, in prisons and in schools of learning.

Pray for God's protection.

Pray for those in authority (Pastors, Ministry Leaders, Community/Political Leaders, Supervisors, and the President).

Pray for peace in the various nations of the world.

Pray that God will bless your hands as He expands your territory for His glory.

Pray for a spirit of thanksgiving in everything.

<u>Prayer Journal</u>

_____
_____
_____
_____
_____
_____
_____
_____
_____
_____
_____
_____
_____
_____
_____
_____
_____
_____
_____
_____
_____
_____

<u>Day 23</u>

<u>Prayer & Scripture</u>

Psalm 9:10

And they that know thy name will put their trust in thee: for thou, LORD, hast not forsaken them that seek thee.

Prayer for Today

Father, in the name of Jesus, thank you for never forsaking me. Your name makes me trust that everything is all right in You.

<u>Daily Prayer List</u>

Pray for your personal relationship with the Lord as your Savior.

Pray for God to fill you with His Presence today.

Pray that God helps you to stay dedicated to His word and to honor His commandments by keeping His word.

Pray that your resources will be used for God's glory.

Pray to serve God throughout your day and through the opportunities that He provides.

Pray for your family, friends and the people you work with and meet.

Pray about everything that you are involved with throughout your day.

Pray for people needing healing and deliverance.

Pray for people in the mission fields, in prisons and in schools of learning.

Pray for God's protection.

Pray for those in authority (Pastors, Ministry Leaders, Community/Political Leaders, Supervisors, and the President).

Pray for peace in the various nations of the world.

Pray that God will bless your hands as He expands your territory for His glory.

Pray for a spirit of thanksgiving in everything.

Prayer Journal

_____

_____

_____

_____

_____

_____

_____

_____

_____

_____

_____

_____

_____

_____

_____

_____

_____

_____

_____

_____

_____

<u>Day 24</u>

<u>Prayer & Scripture</u>

Psalm 34:8

O taste and see that the LORD is good: blessed is the man that trusteth in him.

Prayer for Today

Father, in the name of Jesus, You are good to my taste. Every thing about You is sweetness to my soul, and it satisfies me.

<u>Daily Prayer List</u>

Pray for your personal relationship with the Lord as your Savior.

Pray for God to fill you with His Presence today.

Pray that God helps you to stay dedicated to His word and to honor His commandments by keeping His word.

Pray that your resources will be used for God's glory.

Pray to serve God throughout your day and through the opportunities that He provides.

Pray for your family, friends and the people you work with and meet.

Pray about everything that you are involved with throughout your day.

Pray for people needing healing and deliverance.

Pray for people in the mission fields, in prisons and in schools of learning.

Pray for God's protection.

Pray for those in authority (Pastors, Ministry Leaders, Community/Political Leaders, Supervisors, and the President).

Pray for peace in the various nations of the world.

Pray that God will bless your hands as He expands your territory for His glory.

Pray for a spirit of thanksgiving in everything.

<u>Prayer Journal</u>

_____
_____
_____
_____
_____
_____
_____
_____
_____
_____
_____
_____
_____
_____
_____
_____
_____
_____
_____
_____
_____
_____

Day 25

Prayer & Scripture

John 15:4-5

4Abide in me, and I in you. As the branch cannot bear fruit of itself, except it abide in the vine; no more can ye, except ye abide in me.

5I am the vine, ye are the branches: He that abideth in me, and I in him, the same bringeth forth much fruit: for without me ye can do nothing.

Prayer for Today

Father, in the name of Jesus, I desire to be attached to You. Without You, I can do nothing. Keep me as a branch, always connected to You, the vine.

<u>Daily Prayer List</u>

Pray for your personal relationship with the Lord as your Savior.

Pray for God to fill you with His Presence today.

Pray that God helps you to stay dedicated to His word and to honor His commandments by keeping His word.

Pray that your resources will be used for God's glory.

Pray to serve God throughout your day and through the opportunities that He provides.

Pray for your family, friends and the people you work with and meet.

Pray about everything that you are involved with throughout your day.

Pray for people needing healing and deliverance.

Pray for people in the mission fields, in prisons and in schools of learning.

Pray for God's protection.

Pray for those in authority (Pastors, Ministry Leaders, Community/Political Leaders, Supervisors, and the President).

Pray for peace in the various nations of the world.

Pray that God will bless your hands as He expands your territory for His glory.

Pray for a spirit of thanksgiving in everything.

Prayer Journal

_____

_____

_____

_____

_____

_____

_____

_____

_____

_____

_____

_____

_____

_____

_____

_____

_____

_____

_____

_____

_____

<u>Day 26</u>

<u>Prayer & Scripture</u>

James 5:16

Confess your faults one to another, and pray one for another, that ye may be healed. The effectual fervent prayer of a righteous man availeth much.

Prayer for Today

Father, in the name of Jesus, make me a person that prays for others continuously. Make me a person who has an effective prayer life.

Daily Prayer List

Pray for your personal relationship with the Lord as your Savior.

Pray for God to fill you with His Presence today.

Pray that God helps you to stay dedicated to His word and to honor His commandments by keeping His word.

Pray that your resources will be used for God's glory.

Pray to serve God throughout your day and through the opportunities that He provides.

Pray for your family, friends and the people you work with and meet.

Pray about everything that you are involved with throughout your day.

Pray for people needing healing and deliverance.

Pray for people in the mission fields, in prisons and in schools of learning.

Pray for God's protection.

Pray for those in authority (Pastors, Ministry Leaders, Community/Political Leaders, Supervisors, and the President).

Pray for peace in the various nations of the world.

Pray that God will bless your hands as He expands your territory for His glory.

Pray for a spirit of thanksgiving in everything.

<u>Prayer Journal</u>

_____

_____

_____

_____

_____

_____

_____

_____

_____

_____

_____

_____

_____

_____

_____

_____

_____

_____

_____

_____

_____

<u>Day 27</u>

<u>Prayer & Scripture</u>

Psalm 91:1

He that dwelleth in the secret place of the most High shall abide under the shadow of the Almighty.

Prayer for Today

Father, in the name of Jesus, I dwell in You. You are my secret place.

Daily Prayer List

Pray for your personal relationship with the Lord as your Savior.

Pray for God to fill you with His Presence today.

Pray that God helps you to stay dedicated to His word and to honor His commandments by keeping His word.

Pray that your resources will be used for God's glory.

Pray to serve God throughout your day and through the opportunities that He provides.

Pray for your family, friends and the people you work with and meet.

Pray about everything that you are involved with throughout your day.

Pray for people needing healing and deliverance.

Pray for people in the mission fields, in prisons and in schools of learning.

Pray for God's protection.

Pray for those in authority (Pastors, Ministry Leaders, Community/Political Leaders, Supervisors, and the President).

Pray for peace in the various nations of the world.

Pray that God will bless your hands as He expands your territory for His glory.

Pray for a spirit of thanksgiving in everything.

<u>Prayer Journal</u>

_____
_____
_____
_____
_____
_____
_____
_____
_____
_____
_____
_____
_____
_____
_____
_____
_____
_____
_____
_____

Day 28

Prayer & Scripture

Philippians 4:19

But my God shall supply all your need according to his riches in glory by Christ Jesus.

Prayer for Today

Father, in the name of Jesus, I thank You for supplying all of my needs. Thank you for being my source.

Daily Prayer List

Pray for your personal relationship with the Lord as your Savior.

Pray for God to fill you with His Presence today.

Pray that God helps you to stay dedicated to His word and to honor His commandments by keeping His word.

Pray that your resources will be used for God's glory.

Pray to serve God throughout your day and through the opportunities that He provides.

Pray for your family, friends and the people you work with and meet.

Pray about everything that you are involved with throughout your day.

Pray for people needing healing and deliverance.

Pray for people in the mission fields, in prisons and in schools of learning.

Pray for God's protection.

Pray for those in authority (Pastors, Ministry Leaders, Community/Political Leaders, Supervisors, and the President).

Pray for peace in the various nations of the world.

Pray that God will bless your hands as He expands your territory for His glory.

Pray for a spirit of thanksgiving in everything.

<u>Prayer Journal</u>

_____
_____
_____
_____
_____
_____
_____
_____
_____
_____
_____
_____
_____
_____
_____
_____
_____
_____
_____
_____
_____
_____
_____
_____

<u>Day 29</u>

<u>Prayer & Scripture</u>

Psalm 20:7

Some trust in chariots, and some in horses: but we will remember the name of the LORD our God.

Prayer for Today

Father, in the name of Jesus, I trust You and it is Your name that I will remember in my time of need.

Daily Prayer List

Pray for your personal relationship with the Lord as your Savior.

Pray for God to fill you with His Presence today.

Pray that God helps you to stay dedicated to His word and to honor His commandments by keeping His word.

Pray that your resources will be used for God's glory.

Pray to serve God throughout your day and through the opportunities that He provides.

Pray for your family, friends and the people you work with and meet.

Pray about everything that you are involved with throughout your day.

Pray for people needing healing and deliverance.

Pray for people in the mission fields, in prisons and in schools of learning.

Pray for God's protection.

Pray for those in authority (Pastors, Ministry Leaders, Community/Political Leaders, Supervisors, and the President).

Pray for peace in the various nations of the world.

Pray that God will bless your hands as He expands your territory for His glory.

Pray for a spirit of thanksgiving in everything.

<u>Prayer Journal</u>

_____
_____
_____
_____
_____
_____
_____
_____
_____
_____
_____
_____
_____
_____
_____
_____
_____
_____
_____
_____
_____
_____
_____

<u>Day 30</u>

<u>Prayer & Scripture</u>

Psalm 63:1-2

1O God, thou art my God; early will I seek thee: my soul thirsteth for thee, my flesh longeth for thee in a dry and thirsty land, where no water is;

2To see thy power and thy glory, so as I have seen thee in the sanctuary.

Prayer for Today

Father, in the name of Jesus, I seek You. I thirst for You and long for Your presence. I thank You for Your glory.

Daily Prayer List

Pray for your personal relationship with the Lord as your Savior.

Pray for God to fill you with His Presence today.

Pray that God helps you to stay dedicated to His word and to honor His commandments by keeping His word.

Pray that your resources will be used for God's glory.

Pray to serve God throughout your day and through the opportunities that He provides.

Pray for your family, friends and the people you work with and meet.

Pray about everything that you are involved with throughout your day.

Pray for people needing healing and deliverance.

Pray for people in the mission fields, in prisons and in schools of learning.

Pray for God's protection.

Pray for those in authority (Pastors, Ministry Leaders, Community/Political Leaders, Supervisors, and the President).

Pray for peace in the various nations of the world.

Pray that God will bless your hands as He expands your territory for His glory.

Pray for a spirit of thanksgiving in everything.

<u>Prayer Journal</u>

_____
_____
_____
_____
_____
_____
_____
_____
_____
_____
_____
_____
_____
_____
_____
_____
_____
_____
_____
_____
_____
_____

Day 31

Prayer & Scripture

John 1:12

But as many as received him, to them gave he power to become the sons of God, even to them that believe on his name:

Prayer for Today

Father, in the name of Jesus, I receive You as my Savior. Thank you for making me Yours. I belong to You and You belong to me. I am Your child.

<u>Daily Prayer List</u>

Pray for your personal relationship with the Lord as your Savior.

Pray for God to fill you with His Presence today.

Pray that God helps you to stay dedicated to His word and to honor His commandments by keeping His word.

Pray that your resources will be used for God's glory.

Pray to serve God throughout your day and through the opportunities that He provides.

Pray for your family, friends and the people you work with and meet.

Pray about everything that you are involved with throughout your day.

Pray for people needing healing and deliverance.

Pray for people in the mission fields, in prisons and in schools of learning.

Pray for God's protection.

Pray for those in authority (Pastors, Ministry Leaders, Community/Political Leaders, Supervisors, and the President).

Pray for peace in the various nations of the world.

Pray that God will bless your hands as He expands your territory for His glory.

Pray for a spirit of thanksgiving in everything.

<u>Prayer Journal</u>

<u>Day 32</u>

<u>Prayer & Scripture</u>

Acts 12:5

*Peter therefore was kept in prison: but prayer was made
without ceasing of the church unto God for him.*

Prayer for Today

*Father, in the name of Jesus, I thank You that when the
saints pray on one accord, You meet their desires.*

<u>Daily Prayer List</u>

Pray for your personal relationship with the Lord as your Savior.

Pray for God to fill you with His Presence today.

Pray that God helps you to stay dedicated to His word and to honor His commandments by keeping His word.

Pray that your resources will be used for God's glory.

Pray to serve God throughout your day and through the opportunities that He provides.

Pray for your family, friends and the people you work with and meet.

Pray about everything that you are involved with throughout your day.

Pray for people needing healing and deliverance.

Pray for people in the mission fields, in prisons and in schools of learning.

Pray for God's protection.

Pray for those in authority (Pastors, Ministry Leaders, Community/Political Leaders, Supervisors, and the President).

Pray for peace in the various nations of the world.

Pray that God will bless your hands as He expands your territory for His glory.

Pray for a spirit of thanksgiving in everything.

<u>Prayer Journal</u>

Day 33

Prayer & Scripture

John 15:14

Ye are my friends, if ye do whatsoever I command you.

Prayer for Today

Father, in the name of Jesus, I am honored to be Your friend. I enjoy following Your commandments.

Daily Prayer List

Pray for your personal relationship with the Lord as your Savior.

Pray for God to fill you with His Presence today.

Pray that God helps you to stay dedicated to His word and to honor His commandments by keeping His word.

Pray that your resources will be used for God's glory.

Pray to serve God throughout your day and through the opportunities that He provides.

Pray for your family, friends and the people you work with and meet.

Pray about everything that you are involved with throughout your day.

Pray for people needing healing and deliverance.

Pray for people in the mission fields, in prisons and in schools of learning.

Pray for God's protection.

Pray for those in authority (Pastors, Ministry Leaders, Community/Political Leaders, Supervisors, and the President).

Pray for peace in the various nations of the world.

Pray that God will bless your hands as He expands your territory for His glory.

Pray for a spirit of thanksgiving in everything.

<u>Prayer Journal</u>

_____
_____
_____
_____
_____
_____
_____
_____
_____
_____
_____
_____
_____
_____
_____
_____
_____
_____
_____
_____
_____
_____
_____
_____

<u>Day 34</u>

<u>Prayer & Scripture</u>

Psalm 145:8

The LORD is gracious, and full of compassion; slow to anger, and of great mercy.

Prayer for Today

Father, in the name of Jesus, I appreciate Your grace and mercy towards Your people. Thank you for being full of compassion.

Daily Prayer List

Pray for your personal relationship with the Lord as your Savior.

Pray for God to fill you with His Presence today.

Pray that God helps you to stay dedicated to His word and to honor His commandments by keeping His word.

Pray that your resources will be used for God's glory.

Pray to serve God throughout your day and through the opportunities that He provides.

Pray for your family, friends and the people you work with and meet.

Pray about everything that you are involved with throughout your day.

Pray for people needing healing and deliverance.

Pray for people in the mission fields, in prisons and in schools of learning.

Pray for God's protection.

Pray for those in authority (Pastors, Ministry Leaders, Community/Political Leaders, Supervisors, and the President).

Pray for peace in the various nations of the world.

Pray that God will bless your hands as He expands your territory for His glory.

Pray for a spirit of thanksgiving in everything.

<u>Prayer Journal</u>

_____
_____
_____
_____
_____
_____
_____
_____
_____
_____
_____
_____
_____
_____
_____
_____
_____
_____
_____
_____
_____
_____
_____

<u>Day 35</u>

<u>Prayer & Scripture</u>

Romans 12:2

And be not conformed to this world: but be ye transformed by the renewing of your mind, that ye may prove what is that good, and acceptable, and perfect, will of God.

Prayer for Today

Father, in the name of Jesus, I thank You because you are able to change and transform my mind into the image of You.

Daily Prayer List

Pray for your personal relationship with the Lord as your Savior.

Pray for God to fill you with His Presence today.

Pray that God helps you to stay dedicated to His word and to honor His commandments by keeping His word.

Pray that your resources will be used for God's glory.

Pray to serve God throughout your day and through the opportunities that He provides.

Pray for your family, friends and the people you work with and meet.

Pray about everything that you are involved with throughout your day.

Pray for people needing healing and deliverance.

Pray for people in the mission fields, in prisons and in schools of learning.

Pray for God's protection.

Pray for those in authority (Pastors, Ministry Leaders, Community/Political Leaders, Supervisors, and the President).

Pray for peace in the various nations of the world.

Pray that God will bless your hands as He expands your territory for His glory.

Pray for a spirit of thanksgiving in everything.

Prayer Journal

_____
_____
_____
_____
_____
_____
_____
_____
_____
_____
_____
_____
_____
_____
_____
_____
_____
_____
_____
_____
_____
_____
_____
_____
_____

                                        •••
                                        140

<u>Day 36</u>

<u>Prayer & Scripture</u>

Acts 3:1

Now Peter and John went up together into the temple at the hour of prayer, being the ninth hour.

Prayer for Today

Father, in the name of Jesus, I thank You for allowing us to come together and pray in Your place of worship.

<u>Daily Prayer List</u>

Pray for your personal relationship with the Lord as your Savior.

Pray for God to fill you with His Presence today.

Pray that God helps you to stay dedicated to His word and to honor His commandments by keeping His word.

Pray that your resources will be used for God's glory.

Pray to serve God throughout your day and through the opportunities that He provides.

Pray for your family, friends and the people you work with and meet.

Pray about everything that you are involved with throughout your day.

Pray for people needing healing and deliverance.

Pray for people in the mission fields, in prisons and in schools of learning.

Pray for God's protection.

Pray for those in authority (Pastors, Ministry Leaders, Community/Political Leaders, Supervisors, and the President).

Pray for peace in the various nations of the world.

Pray that God will bless your hands as He expands your territory for His glory.

Pray for a spirit of thanksgiving in everything.

<u>Prayer Journal</u>

_____
_____
_____
_____
_____
_____
_____
_____
_____
_____
_____
_____
_____
_____
_____
_____
_____
_____
_____
_____
_____
_____
_____

Day 37

Prayer & Scripture

Psalm 103:2

Bless the LORD, O my soul, and forget not all his benefits:

Prayer for Today

Father, in the name of Jesus, I will not forget Your benefits toward me. I bless You now and always.

<u>Daily Prayer List</u>

Pray for your personal relationship with the Lord as your Savior.

Pray for God to fill you with His Presence today.

Pray that God helps you to stay dedicated to His word and to honor His commandments by keeping His word.

Pray that your resources will be used for God's glory.

Pray to serve God throughout your day and through the opportunities that He provides.

Pray for your family, friends and the people you work with and meet.

Pray about everything that you are involved with throughout your day.

Pray for people needing healing and deliverance.

Pray for people in the mission fields, in prisons and in schools of learning.

Pray for God's protection.

Pray for those in authority (Pastors, Ministry Leaders, Community/Political Leaders, Supervisors, and the President).

Pray for peace in the various nations of the world.

Pray that God will bless your hands as He expands your territory for His glory.

Pray for a spirit of thanksgiving in everything.

<u>Prayer Journal</u>

_____
_____
_____
_____
_____
_____
_____
_____
_____
_____
_____
_____
_____
_____
_____
_____
_____
_____
_____
_____
_____
_____
_____
_____

<u>Day 38</u>

<u>Prayer & Scripture</u>

2 Corinthians 5:17

*Therefore if any man be in Christ, he is a new creature:
old things are passed away; behold, all things are
become new.*

Prayer for Today

*Father, in the name of Jesus, I thank You for being in my
life. You have made me a new creation in You. Thank
you for taking away my old ways and making me new.*

Daily Prayer List

Pray for your personal relationship with the Lord as your Savior.

Pray for God to fill you with His Presence today.

Pray that God helps you to stay dedicated to His word and to honor His commandments by keeping His word.

Pray that your resources will be used for God's glory.

Pray to serve God throughout your day and through the opportunities that He provides.

Pray for your family, friends and the people you work with and meet.

Pray about everything that you are involved with throughout your day.

Pray for people needing healing and deliverance.

Pray for people in the mission fields, in prisons and in schools of learning.

Pray for God's protection.

Pray for those in authority (Pastors, Ministry Leaders, Community/Political Leaders, Supervisors, and the President).

Pray for peace in the various nations of the world.

Pray that God will bless your hands as He expands your territory for His glory.

Pray for a spirit of thanksgiving in everything.

<u>Prayer Journal</u>

_____
_____
_____
_____
_____
_____
_____
_____
_____
_____
_____
_____
_____
_____
_____
_____
_____
_____
_____
_____
_____
_____
_____

<u>Day 39</u>

<u>Prayer & Scripture</u>

Psalm 86:5

For thou, Lord, art good, and ready to forgive; and plenteous in mercy unto all them that call upon thee.

Prayer for Today

Father, in the name of Jesus, I thank You allowing me to call on You. You are good and merciful to me. When I am wrong, You are ready and there to forgive me.

<u>Daily Prayer List</u>

Pray for your personal relationship with the Lord as your Savior.

Pray for God to fill you with His Presence today.

Pray that God helps you to stay dedicated to His word and to honor His commandments by keeping His word.

Pray that your resources will be used for God's glory.

Pray to serve God throughout your day and through the opportunities that He provides.

Pray for your family, friends and the people you work with and meet.

Pray about everything that you are involved with throughout your day.

Pray for people needing healing and deliverance.

Pray for people in the mission fields, in prisons and in schools of learning.

Pray for God's protection.

Pray for those in authority (Pastors, Ministry Leaders, Community/Political Leaders, Supervisors, and the President).

Pray for peace in the various nations of the world.

Pray that God will bless your hands as He expands your territory for His glory.

Pray for a spirit of thanksgiving in everything.

<u>Prayer Journal</u>

_____
_____
_____
_____
_____
_____
_____
_____
_____
_____
_____
_____
_____
_____
_____
_____
_____
_____
_____
_____
_____
_____

Day 40

Prayer & Scripture

Jeremiah 9:23-24

23Thus saith the LORD, Let not the wise man glory in his wisdom, neither let the mighty man glory in his might, let not the rich man glory in his riches:
24But let him that glorieth glory in this, that he understandeth and knoweth me, that I am the LORD which exercise lovingkindness, judgment, and righteousness, in the earth: for in these things I delight, saith the LORD.

Prayer for Today

Father, in the name of Jesus, I understand that knowing You is more important than anything. My trust is not in the things that I can do, but only in what You can do.

<u>Daily Prayer List</u>

Pray for your personal relationship with the Lord as your Savior.

Pray for God to fill you with His Presence today.

Pray that God helps you to stay dedicated to His word and to honor His commandments by keeping His word.

Pray that your resources will be used for God's glory.

Pray to serve God throughout your day and through the opportunities that He provides.

Pray for your family, friends and the people you work with and meet.

Pray about everything that you are involved with throughout your day.

Pray for people needing healing and deliverance.

Pray for people in the mission fields, in prisons and in schools of learning.

Pray for God's protection.

Pray for those in authority (Pastors, Ministry Leaders, Community/Political Leaders, Supervisors, and the President).

Pray for peace in the various nations of the world.

Pray that God will bless your hands as He expands your territory for His glory.

Pray for a spirit of thanksgiving in everything.

<u>Prayer Journal</u>

ABOUT THE AUTHOR

Tony Simmons is the Pastor of Storehouse Ministries for Christ Church of God in Christ (COGIC), a non-profit ministry purposed to meet the spiritual, physical, and emotional needs of the "Total Person". With that in mind, we give glory to God through His Son, Jesus Christ, and are dedicated to serving humanity. Our focus in Ministry is to have men and women live a lifestyle of worshipping God daily. We are connected with the Church of God in Christ under the leadership of the Presiding Bishop Charles E. Blake, and South Central Georgia Jurisdiction Bishop Norman O. Harper.

In addition to being the Servant Leader for Storehouse Ministries for Christ, Pastor Simmons was appointed as the District Superintendent for the King of Salem District in January 2010. He is married to Rachel Simmons, First Lady of Storehouse Ministries for Christ COGIC and District Missionary for the King of Salem District. He is the father of Brandon and Carlton Simmons, who are both musicians of excellence with the ministry.

To learn more information about Pastor Simmons and the Storehouse Ministries for Christ COGIC, you may visit our website at www.storehousecogic.org.

ABOUT KINGDOM JOURNEY PRESS

Kingdom Journey Press, Inc. is a full-service publishing company specializing in providing customized services to support our clients from the conception of an idea to getting HIStory to the masses! Since the time of inception and in conjunction with our umbrella organization, Kingdom Journey Enterprises, we have become recognized globally for our ability to establish a unique presence, while building relationships with partners and clients consisting of current and aspiring writers, and ministry, business, and community organizations.

Our services include:

- ❖ Manuscript Evaluation
- ❖ Coaching for current and aspiring authors
- ❖ Editing
- ❖ Cover and Print Layout Design
- ❖ Print and E-Book Format
- ❖ Copyright and Distribution
- ❖ Marketing and Sales Support

To contact us and to learn more information about our services, we invite you to visit our website at www.kjpressinc.com.

CPSIA information can be obtained at www.ICGtesting.com
Printed in the USA
LVOW082008301212

313809LV00001B/15/P